SKIPTON

A Pictorial Recollection

compiled by J. K. Ellwood

DALESMAN BOOKS

1975

£1.50

The Dalesman Publishing Company Ltd.,
Clapham (via Lancaster), North Yorkshire.

ISBN: 0 85206 310 5

Front cover: A market scene in front of the parish church and castle gatehouse in about 1830.

Back cover: This view of Skipton High Street in 1840 was painted by the Skipton artist, Richard Waller (1811-82). It shows the old market cross in front of the present Barclay's Bank. The cross was removed shortly after the picture was painted.

The blocks for the production of the prints on the covers have been kindly loaned by the Skipton Building Society.

Printed in Great Britain by Galava Printing Co. Ltd.,
Hallam Road, Nelson, Lancs.

Introduction

This album of photographs is intended for all who have an interest in Skipton, whether they are residents, visitors, or students interested in the buildings and development of the town.

I came to live and work in Skipton in 1953 and took up residence at the Brick Hall Inn—a good centre from which to explore the town and surrounding countryside. One of my first observations was the fact that although the shops had changed from time to time, the upper storeys of the buildings appeared to have changed very little.

From this early interest in the town there developed a fascination for collecting old photographs and, along with Dr. R. G. Rowley, who has helped with the historical detail in this album, I made slides which could be used for lecture purposes.

I hope the reader will enjoy searching out other interesting features in the photographs as well as comparing Skipton as it is with Skipton as it was.

The earliest known etchings of Skipton High Street are the Waller print (on the back cover) and the following three etchings, the first of which is a view of the lower part of the High Street as it was in about 1830.

Above: The upper part of Skipton High Street, also in about 1830, with the Red Lion and Thanet's Arms inns on the right and the Bay Horse and King's Arms on the left. Of these, only the Red Lion survives.

Right: The upper part of Skipton High Street about 1840. Tasker's shop (now the Craven Herald) is clearly seen on the left and Skipton's first gas lamp, "Old Gormless", in front of the church gates.

The visitor to Skipton approaching the town from the south-east along the Aire Valley about 1908 would have to cross old Pinder Bridge, which took the traffic over the Leeds and Liverpool Canal. "Clogger" Thompson's shop can be seen on the left side of the bridge. The notices advertise early films at the Temperance Hall, now the Plaza Cinema.

During the period of demolition and reconstruction of the bridge a temporary footbridge was erected for pedestrians, but heavy vehicles had to divert round by Cavendish Street and Swadford Street. The old bridge was only 22 ft. wide. The builder was Braithwaite of Leeds who also built Carleton road bridge over the river Aire. Clerk of Works was Jim Smith of No. 1, Thornton Street.

After completion, the bridge was tested on November 9th, 1910, when three steam rollers and a traction engine were driven over it in both directions. Note the elegant street lamps on the south side of the bridge.

A view from Pinder Bridge of a canal trip for members of the Rechabites Order.

Above: After crossing Pinder Bridge and walking towards the town one would pass the original Unicorn Hotel through the mass of cattle spreading out from the Market in the High Street and then would face the old Ship Hotel (opposite). This was demolished 1888-90 to widen the narrow and dangerous Ship Corner.

SHIP HOTEL

The new Ship Hotel was one of Skipton's residential hotels until it closed in 1924.

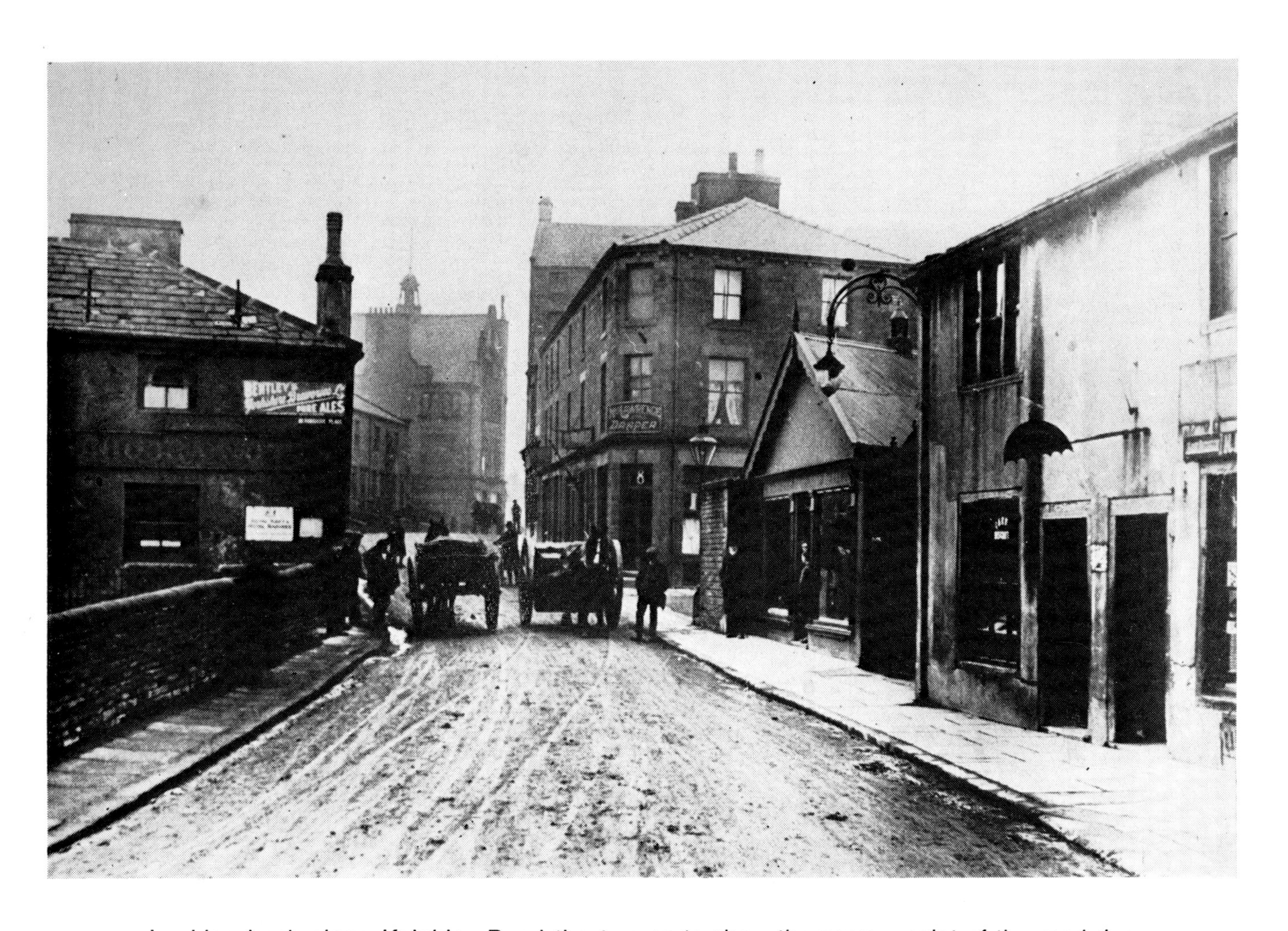

Looking back along Keighley Road the two carts show the narrow point of the road due to the position of the old Unicorn Hotel. They are standing near the entrance to what is now the bus station.

Here we can see the bridge over Waller Hill Beck in Keighley Road which was not widened until the 1920s.

The old Unicorn Hotel was also demolished and rebuilt for road widening purposes.

This shop adjoined the old Unicorn Hotel in Keighley Road on part of the site which is now occupied by the Regal Cinema.

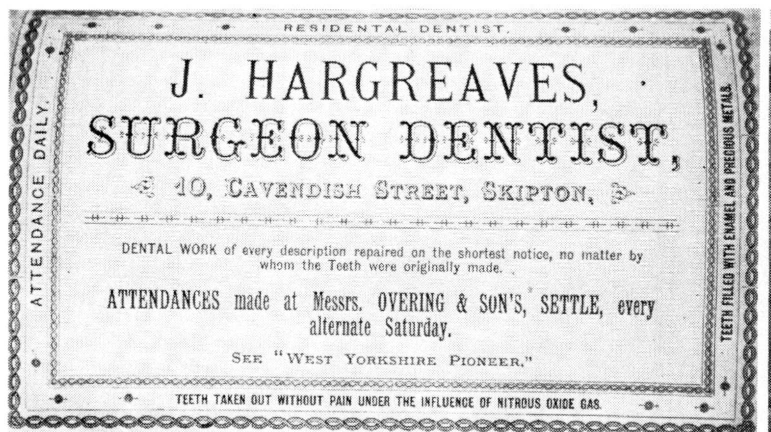

If our visitor had toothache then he need go no further into Skipton. This stately old building was the home of James Hargreaves, the Dentist, who had moved here from premises in Cavendish Street. The house was demolished in 1936 to make way for Burton's Buildings.

John Hogg was landlord of the Ship Hotel from 1874 to 1885. At this time Ship Corner was only 23 ft. wide at its narrowest point. The building on the right was Skipton Post Office. The arch was erected annually in celebration of the Craven Agricultural Society's Show.

Union Square was built in the early 1800s with a top storey specifically provided for hand-loom weaving. Its outer walls now form the supports of the large Union Warehouse occupied by Silentnight (Export) Ltd.

Swadforth, or Swadford Street, is one of the oldest streets, dating back to the 15th Century, the name deriving from a former ford across Eller Beck. This is a view from Belmont Bridge looking towards Ship Corner.

Swadforth House was the home and surgery of Mr. Sloane, the dentist, seen here with his large family at the time of the Coronation of King George V in 1911.

Nearer to Ship Corner, Christ Church Vicarage is on the extreme right. This photograph is dated about 1885-8, the period of the "incumbency" of Francis Addyman, the last landlord of the Ship Hotel before it was demolished.

The old Tithe Barn in its later years was used by travelling showmen and salesmen. It was demolished in 1901 to make way for Mr. A. R. Stockdale's Wine and Spirit Lodge. Originally it had a thatched roof, but this was removed in 1750 and re-covered with stone slates by Mr. Thornton (a founder of the firm, R. Thornton & Sons, Slaters, who are still in business today). This photograph was taken just before the barn was demolished.

Christ Church Vicarage was erected on land given by Skipton Parish Church for the endowment of the new Christ Church erected in 1837. The old Tithe Barn can also be seen on the right. The Vicarage was converted in 1901 to a block of shops now known as Central Buildings.

The Caroline Square aspect of the old Ship Hotel when Francis Addyman was landlord from 1885 to 1888. The Glass, China and Earthenware shop on the right was owned by Mr. Porri. Christ Church Vicarage can be seen in the distance.

Saddler Wilson's shop and the Brick Hall Hotel (once the Devonshire Arms) adjoin the rebuilt Ship Hotel.

Looking at Central Buildings through Ship Corner arch commemorating the Coronation of King George V in 1911.

The High Street was full of activity of a type to which we are not accustomed today when this photograph was taken about 1900. The Midland Bank seen on the right of the photograph was erected in 1888 and next door one can see the Wheatsheaf Inn which closed its doors in 1908. Exchange Buildings seen on the left of the picture were built in 1896 by Mr. C. E. Lowcock, a tailor who occupied the entire building.

The lower section of Middle Row (now Exchange Buildings) about 1875. The three shops were occupied by Andrew the ironmonger, the Craven Pioneer and "Staffordshire House" which was John Metcalfe's furniture and china shop.

Skipton's fortnightly cattle fair was held in the main streets every alternate week until 1906, when after thirty years of argument it was moved to Jerry Croft, now the car park at the rear of the Town Hall.
Within two years of the market moving out of the streets three High Street Inns had closed—the Thanet's Arms, the Fountain and the Wheatsheaf (seen in this photograph).

The state of the streets on wet market days was one of the reasons which led to the agitation for the removal of the market from them. Skiptonians would not go shopping on market days and what the innkeepers gained the shopkeepers lost.

Left: 100 High Street, now the Provincial Building Society offices. William Hogg had a fish, fruit, game and ice shop there from 1892 to 1903. Right: 90 High Street—William Mattock the Corn Merchant was here and down the steps was Mrs. Keighley's eating house. W. Mattock also had the High Corn Mill.

Above: Here at the east end of Newmarket Street stands Billy Gellin, a well known Skipton character who made a living by scavenging coal from the Leeds and Liverpool Canal. Opposite: The old stage coach road from York came down a steep hill known as Shode Bank now Short Bank Road.

In Newmarket Street, until recently, were the premises of Frearson the ironmonger. Philip Walden, the antique dealer, is here now. The Skipton Building Society occupied the adjoining building towards the right of the photograph.

The whole of this south side of Newmarket Street has now disappeared. Among the shops stood a once stately mansion known as Newmarket House (a three storey building) which ended its days as a model lodging house.

The earliest known photograph of Skipton shows the High Street on the occasion of Skipton Show, the annual exhibition of the Craven Agricultural Society, which was held from 1855 to 1929.

An unusual view of the High Street, rarely seen today, before the advent of motor traffic. The first motor car came through the town in 1897. The building on the extreme right was occupied from 1874 to 1895 by Edward Brumfitt who was a cabinet maker. It now forms part of High Street House.

People throng the High Street to celebrate the Coronation of Edward VII on August 9th, 1902.

Caroline Square at the foot of the High Street was the home of Skipton's bus station in the 1920s (above) and 1930s (opposite).

ILKLEY
LEEDS
KEIGHLEY
CLITHEROE
73
SHORT BANK ROAD

The south side of Caroline Square, named after the unhappy wife of King George IV, shows the entrance to Queen's Court. Foster Horner, painter and plumber, was at this shop from 1891 to 1973. "Tinner" Wear was at the adjoining shop. Woolworths now occupy the left hand half of these buildings.

The "original" Fattorini's Corner was erected in 1863 by Mr. Baldisaro Porri for his son-in-law Mr. Innocent Fattorini the jeweller. The adjoining property was demolished in 1895 and now forms part of High Street House.

Nonconformists assembled, banners aloft, in Caroline Square at the conclusion of the annual Whit Monday walk.

John Metcalfe's furniture shop on Sheep Street Hill was demolished in 1895 to make way for Exchange Buildings now occupied by the National Westminster Bank. Temperance speakers used to address the inhabitants from the top of the steps.

Sheep Street before the first world war. Some of the fine shop frontages in the street are shown on the following three pages.

Lipton the grocer displays a mouth-watering selection of fare in an era long before the coming of the supermarket. The placards read: "No Butter like Lipton's: Perfect Quality".

William Stockdale opened a grocer's shop at No. 4 Sheep Street in 1820. From 1892 the firm was Stockdale & Helm which retained the business until 1955.

Phillip the butcher and G. H. Mason the plumber occupied these shops on the site of the old Black Bull Inn, later the Sun Inn. The shops were demolished and rebuilt for G. H. Mason & Son in 1928 and are now occupied by Boots Chemists.

The oldest family business in the High Street is Fred Manby & Bro., established here in 1817. Lower down Middle Row is seen the Fountain Inn, now Dorothy Ward's.

After the first world war Manby's had a garage and motor cycle repair shop at their Union Street premises. They also sold vehicles and one of their first customers was Mr. W. Wiseman who founded "Owd Bill Motors" and can be seen in another rôle later in this book.

This was the first motor car to be built in Skipton at Manby's garage. It is believed that a set of plans was used from a popular mechanics' magazine.

On 27th April, 1897, the Council decided to commemorate the Diamond Jubilee of Queen Victoria by planting the High Street with trees. Mr. George Harrison Mason, who founded the well known firm of G. H. Mason & Sons, was the chairman of the committee responsible for making the arrangements. The lime trees arrived from Carlisle on 9th November, 1897, and planting began on the following day. Here a tree is seen lying on the stone setts awaiting planting.

The trees in the High Street were well established when this photograph was taken of a charabanc outing from the Thanet's Arms Inn about 1907, during the "incumbency" of the last landlord, Mr. H. F. Miller. The last drinks at the Thanet's Arms were served on 23rd December, 1908. The premises are now Messrs. F. A. South, lately Snowden's toy shop.

Until recently Skipton was noted for its many "yards". They were reputed (incorrectly) to have been so laid out as a defence against Scottish incursions. Here is Chancery Lane, so called because it was owned by lawyer Alcock.

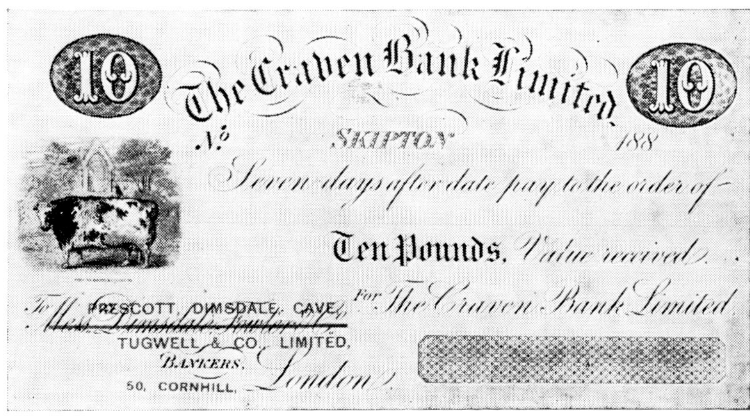

The Alcocks of Skipton and the Birkbecks of Settle were the prime movers in the foundation of the Craven Bank which for many years depicted the Craven Heifer on its bank notes.

Opposite: The High Street photographed from the church tower at 3-40 p.m. (Manby's clock), late 1920s. Above: An earlier photograph of High Street from the same vantage point. In contrast note the lack of motor traffic and the absence of Whitaker's Cafe. Dobson Family Chemist was next door to this property as seen in the photograph overleaf.

The young man in the pony trap is William Wiseman. At this time he was employed by Mr. Dobson, the family chemist, to travel the district for the agricultural side of the business. Another of his duties was to look after Mr. Dobson's personal transport. This shop was until recently occupied by Mr. Murray the chemist and is now a boutique.

William Wiseman later founded Old Bill Motors and opened a garage in Broughton Road.

T. W. HAGAR
DRAPER
MILLINER

Above: The footpath from the church gates to the east side of the High Street, part of which can still be seen in the stone setts above the Town Hall, where the former vicarage stood. This path was raised because of the poor condition of the street, especially on Fair Day.

Opposite: Skipton's annual horse fair was on the decline when this photograph was taken in the early 1930s. It was always held in August following hay-time when the farmers wanted to buy or sell their horses. Some of the horses in this picture, known locally as "July Razors", were owned by the Miller family of Skipton.

Now outside the Public Library, this statue of Skipton's first M.P., Sir Mathew Wilson, Bart., of Eshton Hall, was unveiled by the Marquis of Ripon in 1888. It was unusual for a statue to be erected to anyone in his own lifetime as happened in this case. The house seen in the background (now Dinsdale's shop) was the home and surgery of Dr. Forsyth Wilson and the birthplace in 1882 of his son Charles MacMoran Wilson who was to become Lord Moran, Sir Winston Churchill's personal physician.

Skipton Town Hall with its former canopy and decorated for the Coronation in 1911.

Queen Mary had a great love of antiques and whenever she stayed at Harewood House, the home of the Princess Royal, she enjoyed visiting the most important dealers in the vicinity. Mr. Laycock had a tremendous reputation in the world of antiques, as shown by these two photographs of the Queen's visit to his shop in the High Street about 1930.

LAYCOCK'S
ANTIQ

The north-western entrance to Skipton from Gargrave and Grassington in the early 1900s. The houses which can be seen behind the postman were demolished in 1956.

A view of Salisbury Street before it was extended as Raikeswood Road through to Raikes Road.

Above: The 1911 Coronation procession crossing Mill Bridge.
Opposite: Sandy Goit supplied the water to the High Mill at the entrance to Skipton Woods.

The Round Dam in Skipton Woods, now happily re-opened to the public. The Long Dam and Round Dam were formerly part of the water system for the High Mill and Dewhurst's Mill. These sylvan scenes are within a short walking distance of the busy town centre.

The Springs Canal in spate during the great flood in 1908 when the Round Dam burst its banks following a severe storm.

Two further views of the 1908 floods. Opposite: The scene at Dockyard. Above: The head of Springs Canal. In the top right of the picture can be seen part of the inclined railway which conveyed limestone to the canal from Haw Bank quarries at Embsay.

"Jack Guy's Band", taken about 1890, showing Jack Guy on the extreme right along with others who were to become well known with the Skipton Mission and later Skipton Prize Band. Fred Metcalfe has a white band round his cap and the trombone player near the centre of the top line is A. Clarke. Next to him is Bill Unwin who was a preacher, and next to Dan Champion the drummer is Fred Fowler.

Above: Many members of the band served in the first world war and when they returned some of them soon complained about the name "Mission Band", as they felt that this gave them a poor image when they were off contesting. So in 1919, the name was changed to Skipton Prize Band. In 1927 Fred Metcalfe took them to Crystal Palace where they won the Daily Mirror Trophy.

Right: Fred Metcalfe was the most famous of all the Skipton Band conductors. He was a member of the Skipton Mission in which the band had its roots. He was quite a young man when he was appointed tutor and bandmaster, a position he held until his death in 1930. Here he is seen with "young Fred", his son, Fred Lloyd Metcalfe, who succeeded his father as conductor serving the band well for many years, and now at the age of 80 is one of the best supporters of the Skipton Band as it is today.

When Otley Street was opened out in the early 1840s, the first building to be erected was the Albion Inn which took over the licence of the old Butcher's Arms Inn in Spring Gardens, Otley Road. In common with most of the inns of Skipton it passed into the hands of Scott and Robinson's Skipton Brewery.

Another horse drawn transport was the Skipton steam fire engine, seen here in about 1910 in front of the Black Horse Hotel. The site of this hotel is reputed to have housed the Royal Mews of Richard, Duke of Gloucester (later King Richard III), when he was lord of the Honour of Skipton in 1476-1485.

The garage of the Craven Motor Company in the 1920s. A supermarket now occupies this site next to the Craven Herald.

This was the first Primitive Methodist Chapel from 1835 to 1880. Later, it housed Bishop & Schroot's cycle shop and then was until 1974 the home of Skipton Fire Station.

This De Dion Bouton owned by Dr. Liversidge is seen in front of the Castle Gate.

Opposite: The Red Lion is the oldest inn in Skipton if not in Craven. It is reputed to stand on the site of the former hospital of St. Mary Magdalene, a leper hospital in 1310-50, and is said to have been an inn ever since.

Above: Through the gateway one met this attractive view of the old castle, with the Tudor wing attached. The wing was specially built as a residence for Henry Lord Clifford on his marriage with Lady Eleanor Brandon, grand-daughter of King Henry VII.

EMSLEY
GROCER
PROVISION
MERCHANTS
RED-LION
EMSLEY

Acknowledgements

I am grateful to Frank Knowles who has helped with the copying of the photographs, bringing out details which were hardly noticeable in the originals.

My thanks are also due to the following who have either loaned photographs or have given information about Skipton in days gone by:

J. Inman, D. Armitage, Mrs. M. S. Hargreaves, Mrs. Laycock, Miss Smith, G. Walker, P. Baldwin, G. Throup, F. Manby, D. Manby, F. L. Metcalfe, F. Fowler, C. Wiseman, H. Horner, S. Throup, H. Thurlow, P. Walden, Mrs. Aldridge, Mr. Brumfitt, W. Foster, R. Thornton & Sons, Dr. A. Raistrick and Mrs. J. Horner.

Miss Smith is the daughter of J. H. Smith, the photographer, who took many of these photographs between 60 and 80 years ago. His first studio was on Waller Hill.

People have been very generous in allowing me to copy old and often rare photographs and I apologise if I have omitted anyone from these acknowledgements.